Bold Business Divas Series™

WHAT EVERY DIVA MUST KNOW ABOUT STARTING HER OWN BUSINESS

The Modern Woman's Guide
to Building a Fabulous Brand
From Scratch

CHERYL A. PULLINS
CherylPullins.com

CPI Media

We share your message with the world

What Every DIVA Must Know About Starting Her Own Business
Copyright © 2013 by Cheryl A. Pullins

All rights reserved. No part of this book may be reproduced or transmitted in any form or by any means without written permission from the author.

ISBN-10: 0-9859554-3-0
ISBN-13: 978-0-9859554-3-4

Printed in USA

Cover Image: Theresa NeSmith Photography
Publisher: CPI Media
Layout & Design: CPI Media

Dedication

*To my best friend of seventeen years, Janice,
It is because of you that I stand in the gap
and hold a space for every woman with a
dream.*

*To every woman in the world with a dream of
business ownership, through this book it is
my prayer that you
receive the foundation you need
to live your dream,
rock your awesome,
become the change
and create the change you
want to see in the world.*

Table of Contents

Foreword 11
Re-inventing DIVAS 13
What I Know 15
Know Your Value 21
Know Your Why 25
Know Your Mission 29
Know Your Industry 33
Know Your Peeps 35
Know Your Available Resources 39
Know What You Need to Get Started 42
DIVAS Doing Business Startup Checklist 46
Know How to Prepare 50
Know How to Build a Stellar Brand 53
Know How to K.I.S.S. in Public 59
Know How to Create Systems 61
Know How to Integrate Business and Life 70
Know Your DIVA-NOMIC$ 75
One Vision, Multiple Streams 79
Know How to DIVA-fy Your Image 83
DIVAS Resource List 90
DIVAS Recommended Reading List 93

About the Author

Cheryl Pullins

Cheryl is no stranger to adversity. Adopted at the age of two, shot by a stray bullet when she was just nine, found out her neighbor's children were her younger siblings when she was 12 years-old, met her biological mother at the age of 18, married to a pastor for 14 years before enduring a bitter divorce and child custody fight, Cheryl knows what it takes to overcome and transform lives because she started with her own.

An award-winning international speaker, TEDx Speaker, masterful mentor to women, and passionate advocate for anyone in the midst of extraordinary chaos, loss, grief, and reinvention, Cheryl knows it's the momentary bumps and bruises we hit when we reach rock bottom that give us the strength, courage, and conviction to pick ourselves up, dust ourselves off, and move on.

After working as a corporate Human Resources professional for more than 20 years, Cheryl is now the owner of an internationally recognized boutique personal branding agency, Iconic Persona™ and Creator of the Momentum Coach Certification Program.

With her signature red lipstick and stilettos, Cheryl has been dubbed by her clients as the "Icon of Branding." She is not only a Personal Branding Strategist, but Cheryl is also an award-winning international speaker, TEDx speaker, author, and serves as a mentor for the London-based Cherie Blair Foundation for Women in Business.

Having left the corporate world during the height of her career which included working for an international Silicon Valley-based company, Cheryl now uses her voice to carry the message of economic empowerment for women. In addition to being the author of, *What Every Diva Must Know About Starting Her Own Business*, her second book, *ICONIC: Personal Branding for Women* will soon be released.

Aside from her fascination with fashion, film, and Italian food, Cheryl uses her proven signature personal branding methodology to help seven-figure women business owners, coaches, consultants, and industry leaders to master their message, create their own platform, and make meaningful money while helping more people.

Foreword

Being an entrepreneur is an American dream. Becoming a woman entrepreneur is more of a reality now than ever before. Most women, because they are really good at what they do, believe they can just "jump in" and become a top-notch entrepreneur. Reading this book will help you to become more successful as you begin on your road to success.

There are tremendous truths to the outcomes that you will have by sitting down and using the strategies in this book and putting them into practice. A number of strategies in this book are some of the basic ones which many women entrepreneurs seem to leave out and later wonder why they are not experiencing success. This book puts the basic steps to becoming successful back to the forefront where they belong. The strategies outlined are easy to understand and implement, using focus; drive; passion and vision.

As you start your business journey, this book will also help to make it fun; exciting and most important; obtainable. The principles outlined are proven, necessary and will cause success in your business and life. Leaving out any one of the principles will be like leaving flour out of cake mix. It just won't work.

Suzanne Whitfield

Introduction

Re-inventing DIVAS

She is a woman entrepreneur who:

Is **DETERMINED** to live her dreams.

INSPIRES others to live their dreams.

Knows how to **VALUE** investing in herself.

Has embraced her true and **AUTHENTIC** self.

SUPPORTS the dreams and efforts of other DIVAS.

DIVAS are brilliantly talented and confident women who step out into the world in a bold and big way to serve with their gifts, talents and abilities.

They are aware of their strengths and are in tune with their weaknesses. They are strong and resilient, yet possess a genuine love for those in their sphere of influence.

They are not driven or motivated by money, but they enjoy the finer things of life and understand that money answers all things. They are stylish and chic; full of compassion and grace.

They handle their business and stay abreast of the latest trends to serve their clients with excellence.

DIVAS know the importance of building relationships. They operate from a place of collaboration, not competition, and they know how to celebrate the success of other DIVAS.

DIVAS are highly regarded and respected in their industry and are seen as women of the utmost integrity.

Their family loves and supports their dreams of using their gifts to make a difference in the world.

DIVAS are beautiful on the inside and have hearts full of unconditional love.

Re-inventing DIVAS is about connecting women who are:

DARING

INNOVATIVE

VIBRANT

AWAKENED

SUPPORTIVE

What I Know

There I was. Fresh out of corporate "sing sing."

You see, I had spent more than twenty years on the corporate climb, walking the straight and narrow, staying inside the box. My daily corporate uniform of black, blue, grey, brown and the occasional splash of vixen red, adorned both me and my closet. Pearls and pumps were my Monday through Friday accessories. I didn't break out my favorite, now signature and sassy baubles, until the weekend.

One day, while sitting in my "Corporate America" designated "cell" – my office. It came to me that there had to be more to life than shoving papers from one side of my desk to other, doing pension calculations and managing health benefits for a five billion dollar company. Even in that moment, becoming an entrepreneur wasn't even a thought. Not even a remote one.

For many years I had declared that anyone who wanted to own their own business had to be crazy. Who in the world would want to take that kind of risk, and not even know if you were going to have enough money to operate your business and pay your personal bills?

Oh no, not me, that wasn't my thing. I was a self-proclaimed corporate "lifer." I had worked through the ranks and had begun to establish my presence as a key team member while working for a five billion dollar publically traded company. This little girl from South Philly was doing it. Those years of working and being mentored at that big pharmaceutical company in Philadelphia, while in high school, was now paying off.

All that corporate mumbo jumbo landed me one of the most fun and creative corporate jobs ever.

Downtown San Francisco. One year of living and working in the Bay Area gave me a small glimpse of what freedom felt like. Even though I worked long hours, it was totally acceptable to walk out at three o'clock in the afternoon to the local fancy coffee shop or sit in the park for a strategy session. I was the site manager for a global design firm and having time during the day to clear your head was a whole lot better than feeling like you were in corporate solitary confinement for eight hours a day, five days a week.

Yep. I was living the dream.

Ok, wait. I was living somebody's dream, but it sure wasn't mine. I did not have the dream of California living. But it's an experience I sure wouldn't trade.

There is so much more to this part of the story, but I will save the details for my next book.

But if I could roll back time, just to bring you forward we will go back about ten years, I was in a lost and dark place. I won't give you the blow-by-blow version, but I had reached a place in my life I never knew existed. Something had to change. My life depended on it. The biggest change I embraced was to walk out forgiveness. I realized that I would never experience the "amazingness" of serving humanity with my gifts, if I didn't walk the path of forgiveness, fully and completely.

Once I came through the passage of forgiveness, the floodgates of my life began to open. And one of the biggest waves was becoming an entrepreneur.

May I ask you a few questions? Is there a passion inside of you to start a business, but you have no idea about where to start? How to get started? What to do? Where to go?

If so, then welcome to the club - the passionately clueless club. That's right – clueless.

About three years ago, that was me. I was passionately clueless when I started my business. I knew I had a passion to help women overcome their challenges and obstacles and create an awesome life for themselves, but when I combined that passion with the tactical side of starting a business – I was clueless!

I had no idea about how to market a business, make money or even craft my message in a way that "the right" people wanted to do business with me.

First let me provide full disclosure and share that I never wanted to own a business. You read what I mentioned earlier, entrepreneurship didn't make sense to me. Being an entrepreneur was not "in my blood." I lived by the principle of several myths about business ownership, so I avoided it altogether.

My first venture into entrepreneurship came disguised as a desire to publish a magazine for women. I wanted to create a platform where women could receive information, images, insight and inspiration to live a victorious life.

Victorious living had become personal for me because in spite of everything I had experienced up until that point in my life, I had learned how to live a free life of victory and I wanted to share the experience of living this lifestyle with women – worldwide.

LIVE Magazine became a global sensation. We had readers from across the globe who received inspiration through a digital online magazine that was produced after work hours in the middle of the night, using PowerPoint®.

We featured some of the most notable names in Christian ministry, and as a result, word quickly spread about this life changing magazine for women. But there I was with no strategy or plan for success, and ultimately LIVE Magazine shut its doors.

What I know…

It's not about me, and it's not about you. You are here to contribute to the greater good of humanity. It's not for the big house, the fancy car, the designer clothes or the frequent vacations. You were sent to this earth with gifts and talents encoded in you to serve humanity and to assist with God's bigger vision. It's not about you!

Muhammad Ali said, "Service to others is the rent you pay for room here on earth." My version, "Stop being selfish or your time on this earth will be an empty and unfulfilled experience." Service is your ultimate gift to humanity and the intoxicating feeling of joy you receive by giving that gift is like none other. It's really not about you, but it is about the world that needs what you have in you.

What Every DIVA Must Know About Starting Her Own Business, is my contribution to sharing my experiences, my knowledge and my skill with women around the world who need what I have in me.

This book is a selfless act of sharing my brilliance to help empower you to release yours.

Know Your Value

Having a sense of self worth is the foundation of personal success. Self worth affects your self-image and when you look down on yourself then you will project an image that does not garner respect. Self worth affects and defines your level of confidence, meaning, if you have a high regard for yourself then you will have more self confidence.

Confidence in yourself will help you achieve more things on your own—even those things which you think you are not capable of doing. Aside from this, self worth also dictates your happiness. A woman who is content and satisfied with how her life is will be the happiest woman in the world, and it will not matter what other people think or say.

When you have high self worth, you will be overly concerned about what other people think or have to say about you, because you are confident about who you are as a person, your gifts, your talents and your abilities.

Some people go through their lives without realizing they have a low self-image. Many people are too preoccupied with their everyday struggles that they fail to focus on the most important things, and that is, how to overcome their own challenges and difficulties.

Only you can determine your value, and only you can teach people how to treat you.

Exercise:

Now is a great time to use your journal and write the answers to these questions. Be brutally honest with yourself.

As simple it sounds, not knowing how to define yourself worth could mean you have not considered it in your life.

Q1: What is self worth to me and how important is it to me that I value myself or not?

Your answer to these questions will have a significant impact on your life.

Q2: Do I value myself?
Q3: Who am I as a woman?
Q4: Do I understand what self worth means for me?
Q5: What is my true worth?
Q6: Do other people will put a high value on me?
Q7: How I have taught people to treat me?

Fill in my G.A.P. (Goals Action Plan)

What changes do I need to implement?

What outcomes will I have in the next 30 days as a result?

Know Your Why

It took me a while to find my rhythm to write this chapter. I made several attempts, but for some reason I just couldn't find my authentic space where the truth of my why would flow.

The day I wrote this part, earlier in the day I had gone to Washington, DC to meet with one of my coaching clients. The drive is about forty-five minutes from my house, and I used it as an opportunity to reflect on some things.

While driving, my mind began to wander and I started thinking about my best friend of seventeen years, Janice.

When I met Janice she had been recently widowed and I was going through a nasty divorce. Our children went to the same school, which is how I met her. We developed one of the most amazing friendships an individual could have. It was my first experience of having a friendship where there was absolutely no judgment, just genuine care and love.

Our friendship was such that we had a pact, if one had money, the other had money.

During the course of our friendship my life began to change and I made significant changes and started on my path to understanding my purpose and how I fit into God's bigger plan.

I wanted Janice to go with me and grow with me. But that didn't happen. I made a couple unsuccessful attempts at getting her to assess where she was in her life and had committed to helping her move beyond where she was to where she really wanted to be in her purpose and life.

The last time I hung out with Janice was July 2010. My husband and I were living in Florida and she came to the area to attend a conference. We planned to spend a day together, and we did.

During our time together I brought up the conversation about moving her life forward. She tried to avoid talking about it, but I wouldn't let her. I wanted her to hear my heart, and I wanted her to know she had a bigger purpose for living. It was no secret we both knew she wasn't living to her fullest.

That day she heard my heart and agreed that she needed to make some adjustments if she was going to live to life to her fullest potential.

Three months passed. It was time for Janice to celebrate her fiftieth birthday. The weekend before her birthday her son threw her a big celebration. She had hit the milestone age of fifty. We had our usual text messaging banter. She said she would call me the next day. She didn't.

The day after she was supposed to call me I received a message from her cousin to call. My friend Janice had died in her sleep two days after her fiftieth birthday.

I was devastated. Not only had I lost my best friend of seventeen years, I knew something that many didn't know – she never lived the life she truly desired.

Knowing she had so much potential and that she knew she had never reached her full potential, it broke my heart.

You may be wondering, why I shared this story. During my drive to Washington, DC I connected with my true why.

Yes, I have a desire to have things, experience things and make a difference in the lives of women, but it is on a much deeper level than I initially realized.

My massive global why is that I want to do everything I can to empower every woman I can reach to live to their fullest potential. I will share my gifts, my talents and my abilities to mobilize women to get started and take action now. Don't put your dreams off for another moment. Don't wait until perfect. Perfect will never come. Now is the time. This is your time. Seize every moment and opportunity to live your dreams.

My why is bigger than things and much greater than stuff. It is motivated by the death of my best friend of seventeen years who took her dreams to her grave, and driven by my passion to do what I can to ensure that no woman is left behind.

EXERCISE:

What's my why?

Know Your Purpose/Mission

Don't just live life, but experience life in all its magnificence and splendor, after all, you only get one. And in living this one life becoming clear about why you are here is the foundation to serving through entrepreneurship. It's not enough to have a business, but a business with a purpose that is the answer to someone's problem and serves a greater need in the earth.

In order to get clear and create your *Personal Mission Statement,* start with answering these questions:

- Why am I on earth at this time?
- What is my mission?
- What is my purpose?

Don't get flustered. Remember, it's personal. Many times we know why we are here, but we don't take the time to write it down and create a plan to execute its mission.

Did you know that 97% of people live their entire life without writing a personal mission statement? And a large majority of them never live their ideal life. The top 3% are the achievers who live their dreams. Don't you want to be a part of the top 3% who are living their dreams, instead of the 97% of those who live average lives?

In his book, *7 Habits of Highly Effective People*, Stephen Covey shares Habit #2: Begin with the end in mind.

Create your Personal Mission Statement - begin with the end. You can't effectively create goals if you don't know your mission or purpose. If you don't take the time to develop a blueprint for why you are here on this earth, then you are just wasting time and breath. It might sound harsh, but it's true.

To help craft a *Personal Mission Statement,* answer these questions:

- What skills do I have?
- What is my passion?
- Who do I serve?
- What is their problem?
- What is the result of my solution?
- What value do I want to I create?

Fill in my G.A.P. (Goals Action Plan)

What changes do I need to implement?

What outcomes will I have in the next 30 days as a result?

Know Your Industry

Taking time to research your industry means you have at least figured out the type of business you are starting. Knowing Your Industry is critical to the success of your business. It is not as simple as doing an Internet search. While Internet research is a part of your process, before beginning you need to have a list of specific questions about your industry to guide your search.

A good way to conduct your research is to create a research worksheet. This worksheet should list the questions that will help you build the proper foundation for starting and/or growing your business.

What type of questions should you consider?

- Industry size
- Industry growth rate
- Future industry growth
- Leading products and services in the industry
- Profit potential
- Key industry trends
- Client needs
- Major industry players
- Industry gaps

Be thorough and specific, but don't get caught up in the research. Get in, get what you need to make solid decisions and move forward.

Fill in my G.A.P. (Goals Action Plan)

What industry research do I need to do?

What outcomes will I have in the next 30 days as a result?

Know Your Peeps

Clearly identifying your ideal client is a critical component to the success of your marketing efforts and more involved and detailed than most entrepreneurs expect. Entrepreneurs typically hit the following top five areas to determine what their ideal client looks like:

- Age
- Gender
- Income
- Location
- Industry

However, in reality, just using those demographics provides access to a much broader audience. Your ideal client has specific needs and their look and feel will be specific, as well. One of the best ways to set your brand apart from the herd is to abandon "cookie cutter" offerings to your market. Creating an *Ideal Client Profile* will help guide you in crafting signature products your market will need.

Defining your ideal client creates a full scope image of your prospective clients. It includes becoming intimately aware and in tune with exactly how your ideal client looks, their needs, how they think, their goals, where they hang out and what solutions they require to answer their issues.

Crafting an image of your ideal client is a comprehensive study on how to position yourself in the marketplace so they can find you and your product. Not only does having an *Ideal*

Client Profile help you speak directly to them, but it also helps your ideal client identify you as someone who has the solution to their problem.

The chart below is a guide to assist with guiding in you in the information needed to build the foundation to create your *Ideal Client Profile.*

Ideal Client (Peeps) Characteristics

Demographics	*Geographics*	*Psychographics*
Age	Location	Personality
Gender	Local	Magazines
Income	National	Shopping Habits
Marital Status	Global/International	Lifestyle
Industry		

Fill in my G.A.P. (Goals Action Plan)

What changes do I need to implement?

What outcomes will I have in the next 30 days as a result?

Know Your Available Resources

When starting a business you can become overwhelmed with all the available information, sometimes to the point of paralysis.

The Internet provides access to an insurmountable amount of information. You can type in a word or a phrase and get millions of responses in less than two seconds – depending on your connection speed. With this level of access it is easy to forget about other offline resources which may be quite beneficial to a new entrepreneur.

Your country area, state or county may have a business development center that provides no cost or low cost business classes. Some areas have local resource centers who support small businesses. If you are in the United States, you can also find a Score mentor to work with you on certain areas of your business.

Tip: An effective Score mentor would be someone with financial or legal experience and knowledge.

Starting a business is not for the faint of heart, but a great way to build a solid foundation and get ahead of the game is to make yourself available to the many resources in your local area.

Fill in my G.A.P. (Goals Action Plan)

What changes do I need to implement?

What outcomes will I have in the next 30 days as a result?

Know What You Need to Get Started

Be realistic about what resources you will need to start your business. No one starts a business with the intention of failing, but statistics have consistently shown that most businesses fail within the first five years - women entrepreneurs, within twenty-four months. This is primarily because they didn't assess what it would take to build the proper foundation for their business.

Building a business requires the same basic mindset for building a house. Building a house requires blueprints, digging the right foundation, installing the plumbing pipes correctly, building out the frame and so forth. Without the proper planning, foundation and building, the house will begin to crack, buckle and eventually fall.

Frequently, entrepreneurs start their business with a logo and a website. They don't put any time into considering what it will take to build a profitable and sustainable business that will outlive them and leave a legacy. You should think of your business as your imprint on the world for generations to come. You want to be known for more than a nice logo and a pretty website, but a failed business.

Some of the areas where you want to be realistic are:
- Your industry
- Start-up costs
- Operational Budget
- Profit Margins

Talk to someone who is already successfully doing what you want to do.

Yes, I admit, this may be a challenging task to accomplish. New entrepreneurs are sometimes shunned by those who are successful in the marketplace; but do not allow that to discourage you. There is a successful entrepreneur in your industry, somewhere, who will take the time to "show you the ropes". Remember it can be more than one entrepreneur.

How can you accomplish this?
- Know the top performers in your industry you want to learn from.
- Have a list of specific questions you want them to answer.
- Contact them through the proper channels – don't circumvent their contact system; but that doesn't mean you can't be creative in getting their attention.
- Be open to communicating with them through email.

Tip: Set up Google Alerts to keep up to date on the successful entrepreneurs you want to learn from. This helps you to stay connected to the conversations happening about the person. Plus it shows you have been studying them prior to contacting them.

Fill in my G.A.P. (Goals Action Plan)

What changes do I need to implement?

What results will I have in the next 30 days as a result?

Bold Business Diva
START-UP CHECKLIST

☑ Determine your business structure.

(Solo, LLC, S-Corp, etc).

☑ Secure state business license and government Tax ID/EIN

☑ Open proper business banking accounts

(Check with an attorney, accountant/business tax specialist)

☑ Create a business plan (Especially if you are seeking bank financing)

☑ Secure any required business insurance

☑ File a DBA Name (Doing Business As Name), if desired

☑ Check hosting, email domain names for website

☑ Create the brand – what you promise to deliver

☑ Create a marketing strategy (online/offline) with a budget

☑ Organize and schedule time to work on your business

☑ Take professional headshots for marketing materials – be sure to get photo license from photographer for ownership of your shots

☑ Order business cards

☑ Be sure your marketing strategy includes social media

☑ Identify organizations, sources and networks – helps with where to market/network

☑ Develop a media kit (online and offline)

☑ Research your industry

☑ Get a clear picture of your ideal client

☑ Visit your local Small Business Development Center

☑ Attend at least one (1) intense business boot camp/conference per quarter

☑ Determine your price structure using a formula for profit

☑ Develop your 15-30-second K.I.S.S. Statement

☑ Invest in a coach who can take you to the next level and beyond

☑ Join a mastermind group (virtual or in person)

☑ Get your ego out of the way

☑ Don't stop until you are living your dreams!

Fill in my G.A.P. (Goals Action Plan)

Who do I want to meet in my industry?

What outcomes will I have in the next 30 days as a result?

Know How to Prepare

There is lots of excitement when deciding to start your business. Once the decision was made, I am sure you were ready to jump in and start making money. Right? Of course you were. There are three basic reasons for starting a business:
- You can make your own schedule
- You have a passion to provide a product/service
- You want to make money/live your dreams

But realistically, before you get to the money making part, you want to secure the foundation of your business by putting into place the legal and financial framework for growing a successful and profitable one. These tips are going to read a bit quicker because they are straightforward; but each bears an important distinction, so consider them carefully before making any decisions.

You will need to determine which business structure is best for your business. I recommend going through this process with both a tax and legal professional. In the United States there are more than ten types, but these are the most common business structures.

Note: This information is general in nature and is not to be viewed as legal advice. In other words, get an attorney and a tax professional with knowledge and experience in business structure.

Definitions of business structures:

Sole Proprietor: A business owned by one person, who is entitled to all of its profits and responsible for all of its debts.

Partnership: A business owned by two or more people, who agree to share in its profits.

Limited Liability Corporation (LLC): A hybrid legal form of business that is taxed like a sole proprietorship with the same liability protection of the corporate structure.

Corporation: A legal form of doing business that creates a separate legal entity from the individual owners. This legal entity can act and do business on its own just as a person would.

S Corporation: A type of corporate legal form that is taxed like a sole proprietorship. Its formation is subject to certain legal criteria such as a maximum number of shareholders.

- Secure a Federal Employer Identification Number
- Assemble an operations team: Accountant, Lawyer, and an unbiased, but experienced business owner.
- Secure any required business licensing and insurances required in your country, state, city, and/or county.
- Develop a business plan: This document is usually thought of solely for the purpose of securing financial resources; however, a well developed business plan is an effective way to help you keep pace with the goals of your business and on track for growth.

Fill in my G.A.P. (Goals Action Plan)

What do I need to implement?

What outcomes will I have in the next 30 days as a result?

Know How to Create Your Brand

Now this is where the work – I mean – fun begins.

I chose to pair branding and marketing together because there is a huge misconception, especially with newbie entrepreneurs, that they are the same thing and you don't have to do both.

They are different, and yes you do!

Let's briefly explore the truth, the differences, and the need for branding and marketing as well as how they work in tandem to help build your stellar brand.

Promise + Identity + Personality + Influence
=
Branding

Branding is building a reputation that influences emotion which results in a decision to buy the brand. It says that you will deliver what you say. **It's the promise.**

Marketing = Interest

Marketing is creating a perceived value to get buyers to purchase. In marketing, it is more about the psychology of the purchase.

Branding and marketing are not just about logos or websites, but about influence and interest.

How does this relate to and impact your business?

As an entrepreneur, branding and marketing are vehicles or pathways used to communicate your influence and hear the market's interest in your business. No business can survive or be successful without building a reputation of delivering what they promise and creating interest in a product/service that sells.

Branding and marketing are the lifeblood of your business.

I love the basic definition of brand. It means "to burn". Burn the image of your business into the mind of your market and follow up with marketing.

As an entrepreneur there are a few things to get you started with developing your brand and building a strategic and effective marketing campaign. However, before you jump into the deep water there are some simple and effective ways to get your business name into the marketplace by creating your identity and gaining market interest.

- Develop a 15-30-second Impact Statement that explains who you are, what you do and who you do it for. It's the K.I.S.S.
- Please please please, if I don't stress anything else, have professional photos done. Please. Stop using unprofessional photos to represent your brand in the marketplace. Visuals are part of the brand experience. Unprofessional images do a disservice to your brand and they do not represent you well in the marketplace. Actually, they act as a repellent.

You don't have to break the bank, but you do have to make the investment.
- Identify online and offline networking organizations and forums to build relationships.
- Create a social media strategy for networking and engaging. Don't just hang out on Facebook and Twitter, or any social media platform just for the heck of it. Put some purpose in that party and build a strategy so it rolls up to your bottom line.
- Work with a branding and marketing professional. Your brand and business are both worth the investment.

Ways to Amplify Your Brand Voice (Offline & Online)

Social Networks	Website
Professional Associations	Newsletter
Groups	Digital Magazine
Social Events	Joint Ventures
Charity Events	Warm Letters
Blogs/Guest Blog	Forums
Videos	Conferences
Podcasts	Vendor Opportunities
Civic Groups	
Volunteer Opportunities	
Industry Specific Groups/Events	
Educational Activities	
College Campus	
Expos	
Speaking	
Advertising	
Direct Mail	
Press Releases	
Live Events	
Webinars	
Freebies	

Fill in my G.A.P. (Goals Action Plan)

What do I need to do to expand my brand presence?

What outcomes will I have in the next 30 days as a result?

Know How to K.I.S.S. in Public

6 Simple Steps to Creating Your "Claim to Fame" Statement

Step One: My name is _____

Step Two: Use a KISS (Keep It Simple Statement)
Examples: I am an author. I am a consultant.

Step Three: What do I do?
Examples: I teach, train, lead, create, provide

Step Four: Who do I do it for?
Examples: Gender, Age, Type of person, Occupation

Step Five: What do I help them do?
Use specific terms. Stay away from vague clichés

Step Six: To get what result?
Again, be specific.
Examples: To increase, To focus on, To build profitable

Know How to Create Systems

Edwards Deming, a statistician who was credited with bringing quality control to Japan and also revolutionized United States business practices, said "Ninety-seven percent of business failure is due to the system."

You may be wondering, "What is a system?" Just in case you are, let me explain.

Systems help to create order out of what can become chaos. If I can be formal for just for a moment, a system is a package of processes that deliver the same result. It's the organization of functional interactive units for the achievement of a common goal.

In simple terms: a system is a consistent way of doing the same thing and getting the same result. For business purposes, a system is a repeatable process that produces a profit.

A common example of a system at work is a fast food restaurant drive-thru. They have a system in place for you to get your food without leaving your car, and still produce a profit. This system produces a win-win.

That is if they get your order right!

"Fast Food" DIVA

Recently I started this pretty bad habit of stopping at the drive-thru around the corner from our house on my way home from church. It's usually about one o'clock in the afternoon and my husband and I both are usually hungry. We take separate cars to church because he has to be there ninety minutes before service begins, and I am just not a morning person and I have no interest in sitting around for ninety minutes before service starts.

Since starting these "golden arches" runs my husband has become accustomed to them. "Gotta" break that habit quick, but those trips have allowed me to take a closer look at the pretty well oiled fast food drive-thru system.

The drive-thru system is a part of many fast food operations, and if you look closely, it's quite simple.

You drive up, hopefully knowing what you want to order; speak into the little speaker box and drive to the next window to pay. Then you either wait for them to hand you your food or you drive to the next window to get your food. You can have all of this done in less than three minutes.

When you think about it, wouldn't you want your business to operate this way, where all the moving parts are in sync without your having to show up in the office every day trying to do everything, and still produce a profit?

Why have systems in your business?
- Systems allow for growth.
- Provide for increased productivity for both you and your staff.
- Gives you a leveraged capacity to serve more people.
- Enables you to hire and train easily.
- Can put your business on auto-pilot and give you the freedom you want as an entrepreneur

The primary personal purpose of your business should be to serve your life, not for your life to be a slave to your business.

Systems give your business a foundation of consistency and they allow you to the freedom to focus on what you are passionate about – the reason you went into business in the first place – serving your market with your gifts, talents and abilities.

Ways to Systematize Your Business

Marketing System

A major part of being an entrepreneur means having to market your business – regularly and often.

I often coach entrepreneurs that they must "consistently market and market consistently". But in order to do that effectively, you must take the time to create what I call an *Integrated Strategic Marketing* plan which you can systemize over a recurring cycle.

Calendaring System

Activities which you do repeatedly can be done in blocks of time.

Time blocking is dedicating a certain amount of time for a given task. One of the most common tasks entrepreneurs can become overwhelmed and distracted by is email. We all fall prey to the constant email dings and pop-ups. All it takes is one email ding to get you side-tracked from working on a money-making activity and instead follow down the path of the new email. Then before you know it, you are surfing the web in search of airfare deals because the email was from your sister about planning the family reunion and she wants you to find a good fare for mom...yada yada yada. Then somehow you end up in social media land, and you know the rest.

Time blocking gives you a specific amount of time to work on similar type tasks. For example, you can schedule a thirty minute time block two times per day to read and respond to email.

Tip: Set up an email auto response which informs clients that you review and respond to emails twice daily. It helps to set the expectation, while teaching them how to treat you in the process.

The key to time blocking is not to become stressed about not completing the task when time is up. You can pick up where you left off the next time. This will definitely require some mind shifts and changes in behavior and discipline, but you can do it. You will see how much time you get back in order to work on value added and revenue generating activities (REVGAs).

Document your systems

This is a very important part of systematizing your business.

As an entrepreneur, I am sure you have a system for doing everything you do, but no one probably knows about it except you.

Documenting how you do things is key and helps to ensure that your systems and processes are repeated properly and can function without interruption. Writing your systems step-by-step gives you ownership of the process, also known as an operations manual.

Refer back to the fast food example. They have a system in place so that regardless of who does the task, if the correct steps are completed in the correct order, the same result will be achieved.

Michael Gerber, author of *The E-Myth* says, "If you don't write it down, you don't own it."

Own the systematic process for your business.

Prioritize what needs to be systematized.

Key areas you should systematize:
- Financial Systems: Invoicing, Tracking Costs, Cash Flow and Income Statements
- Time Management Systems: Scheduling, Organization, Prioritization, Concentration, Creativity and Product Development
- Client Delivery: Work Flow, Communications, Forms and Proposal Templates
- Marketing Systems: Strategy, Research, Lead Generation and Lead Conversions

Fill in my G.A.P. (Goals Action Plan)

What systems do I need to create in my business?

What outcomes will I have in the next 30 days as a result?

Know How to Integrate Business and Life

You could be thinking, "What do I need to know about my personal and business life that I don't already know?"

Hah! Lots!

The first thing I want you to know is that your business and life are separate, yet together. You are the common denominator. There is one thing for certain, what goes on in your life, show up in your business.

As an entrepreneur you spend a significant amount of time working on your business and unfortunately when first starting, you could be working "in" your business too. When you worked a "regular job" you most likely worked a regular shift of a set number of days and hours – that was it. But now you think, talk, sleep, eat and crave everything having to do with your business, all the time. I know I do. I am sure there are times you think of innovative business ideas at times when you really shouldn't. But it happens, because your subconscious mind is always looking for ways for you to reach your goals, both business and life.

On a daily basis you are working tirelessly to build and market your business and work with your clients; all the while you may also be playing other life roles of wife, mother, caretaker, etc.

But here is where you have to draw the line, so to speak. Be aware of what I call, "Entrepreneurial Spillage." This is where your business spills over into your life and begins to consume it to the point where it takes over. Trust me, if you give your business permission it will take over your life.

A lesson you must learn is that you control the gates on when you answer emails, phone calls and schedule meetings.

For example, I work my business from home and my husband works outside of our home, I schedule most of my business-related activities between 7am and 4pm. Don't get me wrong, I have flexibility in my scheduling because I do serve clients who have full-time jobs in addition to their businesses, but my point is that I don't make it a practice of always working. As a matter-of-fact, there are many Fridays, especially during the summer, where I don't work at all. I use Friday as a day to do whatever I want to do – it's typically my designated me day.

But guess what? You can too.

I digress. I want to touch briefly on your business life. The main point I want to make here is – invest in you.

I see it time and time again where entrepreneurs give the excuse of not having the time or resources to invest in themselves to become the best or the expert in their industry.

You will not grow a thriving or profitable business without first investing in yourself. You must see the value in growing your knowledge and exposing yourself to those who are doing more and are at a higher level than you. Be teachable. Regardless of where you are and what you know, you can learn from anyone.

You cannot expect others to perceive you as the best or the expert if you haven't invested in yourself - at least on the same level you are expecting others to invest in you.

If you are only investing a few dollars here and there to grow your business, it will only grow to the level of your investment. An easy example is gardening. Now, I don't care for gardening personally. I don't like kneeling down and playing in dirt, but it is a good example of investment and growth.

Gardens take work and they can yield a return on investment if taken care of properly. Gardens require water, food, nurturing and regular attention; otherwise you wind up with nothing.

It's the same with you and your business. You must invest not only time, but also resources. Investing in yourself in turn helps to grow your business; just like investing time, energy and resources into a garden gives you beautiful flowers or healthy and nutritious vegetables.

In the end, you, your business and your clients all benefit and receive a return on investment. This is a simple principle of sowing and reaping. If you sow little, you reap little, but if you sow big you reap even bigger.

Okay, let's get back to talking about business and life integration. An imperative part of this section is my 7 Strategies for Business and Lifestyle Integration Management. Sounds fancy, huh? These seven strategies are the foundation upon which you can build, not only a success business, but also a freedom-based lifestyle.

7 Strategies for Business and Lifestyle Integration Management

- Clarify your roles.
- Learn to say "yes" to yourself first.
- Set standards for yourself (rules to live by).
- Establish clear boundaries
- Communicate boundaries.
- Schedule "me time."
- Create a technology free zone

Fill in my G.A.P. (Goals Action Plan)

What changes do I need to implement?

What outcomes will I have in the next 30 days as a result?

Know Your *DIVA-NOMIC$*

It's finally time to have "that" conversation. Yes, we are talking about money. What I like to refer to as *DIVA-NOMIC$*.

In his book, Secrets of the Millionaire Mind, T. Harv Eker shares a series of wealth principles. While the entire book is awesome, this principle is one of my favorites:

"If you want to change the fruits, you must first change the roots. If you want to change the visible, you must first change the invisible."

If I can "Cheryl-ify" it I would say, *"You can only produce the fruit from the seeds you have planted. You can't plant tomatoes and expect to reap corn."*

Before we get into talking about money from a "what you want to earn to live your dreams standpoint," you must first look at your financial fruit and have a candid and honest conversation with yourself about your money relationship. Yes, you have a money relationship and in order to produce the "financial fruit" needed to live the life you love, you must first look at your PMS – Personal Money Story." What do I mean by "Personal Money Story?" I will use mine as an example.

I grew up as an only child. Even though I have five biological brothers and sisters, I was adopted by a much older woman, she had one son and he was old enough to be my father.

In our house we were in a financially decent place. We weren't the Rockefellers, but we were a long way from being "poor." Our family home was paid off, my mom always had a five digit bank balance and I wanted for nothing. This is saying a lot for a single woman, born in 1910 who had migrated from the south to the north with an eighth grade education and created an amazing life for both of us. She was a very successful and influential entrepreneur, which I didn't appreciate until later years – much later.

Eventually, I learned what really motivated her financial success. When it came to money she was driven by the fear of scarcity. She was afraid there wouldn't be enough. Saving money for her was more about the fear of not having enough money than it was about creating a financial legacy. There's a difference.

In spite of being in a pretty good financial place she would often say and I often heard, "we can't afford that." One of the reasons I didn't immediately attend college is because she said, "we can't afford that," and secondly she was successful with an eighth grade education - the investment of college didn't make sense to her.

"We can't afford that," eventually became my mantra and Personal Money Story. I had caught the scarcity mindset bug and sometimes, now, I have to work to not fall back into that self-sabotaging thinking. As an entrepreneur you cannot afford to have your PMS impacting your financial bottom line.

Your Personal Money Story is not about money as much as it is about two things:

1. What you consistently heard and experienced growing up
2. The setting of your internal "Financial Thermostat"

Journal Time Exercise:

1. Write whatever you can recall about money when you were growing up: what you heard, what you experienced, how it made you feel

2. Write how your Personal Money Story has impacted your life

Fill in my G.A.P. (Goals Action Plan)

What financial changes do I need to implement?

What results will I have in the next 30 days as a result?

One Dream, Multiple Streams: Know How to Monetize Your Business

In a nutshell, monetization is taking an idea, concept or intellectual property and converting it to an income stream. You can take one thing and create multiple streams of revenue. Monetization is easier to explain by showing you how it works.

Let's take a sixty-minute presentation created once and see how many different revenue generating streams we can create:

1. Audio – single
2. Video – DVD
3. Six-week group class
4. Home study system
5. Live event
6. eBook
7. Print Book
8. Signature Coaching Program

This is just an example, but this is what is known as repurposed content, also known as "rinse and repeat". You can also break down the same content and use it for blog posts, social media posts, magazine articles and white papers for free gifts for lead generation.

You could be thinking, "I am not a coach. How would monetization work for me?"

I work with hair salon owners, and one of the things I cover is monetizing their knowledge. For example, for one of my clients, I recommended that she do a series of mini-videos for her clients on how to take care of their hair between visits. I suggested that she include step-by-step basics for hair washing, conditioning, overnight care, etc. This is a solution to their problem of not knowing how to properly care for their hair from the time they leave the salon until they return. It maintains the continuity of service provided by the stylist.

My client can now package the video series into a DVD product and create a home care system for purchase. She can take the same information, strip the audio and create CDs. She can use the audio, have it transcribed, add helpful images and turn it into a quick read "how to" book which she can sell or use as a lead generation tool.

See how monetization works? I told you I could show you better than I could tell you!

Exercise:

Take a sheet of paper and draw a line down the middle. Use both sides to brainstorm and come up with at least 50 different ways to generate income. Narrow the list down to your top ten. Then choose 2-3 to implement in the next 30 days.

Fill in my G.A.P. (Goals Action Plan)

What monetization activities will I implement?

What outcomes will I have in the next 30 days as a result?

Know How to *DIVA-fy* Your Image

A Bold Business Diva is identifiable by specific traits and an immediate first impression demeanor which makes her someone others want to not only do business with, but be connected to as well.

Many times when people think of the word DIVA, they usually have a negative image or have had a negative experience with someone who has a "diva-esque" attitude. But this book and the Bold Business Diva movement represents something totally different, empowering and refreshing.

DIVA-fying your image enables you to become part of a movement of women who are:

DETERMINED to live their dreams

INSPIRES others to live their dreams

VALUES investing in themselves, and others

Has embraced their **AUTHENTIC** self

Using the word I-M-A-G-E as a guide, there are five key strategies you can use to create a *DIVA-fied* image that is magnetic, irresistible and expresses not only how extraordinary you are, but that you are serious about doing business.

Image is more than how you look and what you wear. Your image starts on the inside and is enhanced by how you adorn yourself on the outside. With that being said, it is your external image which gives the initial impression and communicates in less than twenty seconds. The question you must ask yourself is, "What does my image communicate?"

I – First **IMPRESSION**
M – **MODEL** Excellence
A – Be **APPROACHABLE**
G – Exude **GRACE**
E – You Are **ENOUGH**

First Impression: As simple as this term may sound, the concept of *first impressions* is steeped in psychology. Not to get too far into the way people think, but first impressions are derived from the cognitive unconscious. In short, we see, we unconsciously comprehend and then decide whether or not we like what we just saw – in a matter of nano seconds.

With this in mind, as a woman entrepreneur, it is imperative that you create the image of how you want to be perceived and received in the marketplace. If you want to be taken serious, you must show up like you are ready to do business. I'm not just talking about your outfit and accessories, but I am also referring to showing up wearing self confidence, ready to step out of your comfort zone and into your power, with a strong sense of who you are and the unique value you bring to the world.

Model Excellence: There are many who have their eyes on you, watching, waiting and hoping that you do one of two things – fail or succeed. The freedom of knowing this is that neither should impact the level of your output nor being a shining example of excellence.

Modeling excellence should be seen in both the business and personal sides of your life. When you show up as a woman who models excellence, you then become the example of who others aspire to emulate.

I always consider it a compliment and a testament to the excellence I strive to model, when someone duplicates something I have created or developed. Many entrepreneurs – especially "newbies" – get frustrated when they see that someone has copied their idea. But I am of the opinion that there is nothing new under the sun, and that in spite of what appears to be a duplication of ideas, no one can copy, duplicate or steal the authenticity and vision you bring. As you model excellence others will model you. Embracing this truth will save you heartache, headache and will keep you from watering down your brand by looking like a woman who whines. I know it's harsh, but watch successful brands, you don't see them complaining about someone "taking their stuff." Wendy's, McDonald's and Burger King all make hamburgers using their own unique brilliance. It's not what you do as much it is about how you do it, and no one can emulate your brand of "awesome!"

Be Approachable: I honestly wanted to talk about being authentic, but since I am talking about image, addressing the issue of being approachable is most appropriate.

I had the experience of meeting someone I had been admiring from a distance for quite some time. We both attended an event and I was tickled pink when I noticed they were standing about ten feet from me. With eager excitement I proceeded to walk towards the amazing woman I had admired for so long. The closer I got she sensed that I was walking toward her, and much to my surprise the initial greeting was quite cold in a "why are you bothering me" kind of way. But before I could adjust my excitement, she noticed my name tag and her entire countenance and tone of her voice changed.

Of course in the moment I felt relived, but after giving the situation some serious thought it concerned me. Here was this woman of influence being totally un-approachable. Boy, what a turn off! Yes, I know that once she recognized me as someone familiar her handling of me changed, but what about the women she may not know, who want to greet her? Those women will most likely share a different kind of experience.

DIVA-fying your image means that you are approachable, and in **ready to serve mode**. You do not want to have a reputation for being un-approachable. It will impede your ability to reach those you have been called to serve with your brand, your message and your business.

Grace: This is a great segue from being approachable. Being a woman of grace, I believe, takes a certain mindset. That mindset is that it's not about you. A woman of grace understands that she gains respect through being gracious, kind and compassionate. A woman of grace exudes confidence, yet she considers those around her. She is a woman of influence, yet she doesn't flaunt her ability to motivate. She is styled in grace and adorned in an authentic eloquence that only she can express.

You Are Enough: This is the most critical of them all when it comes to your image, and you must get to this place in your mind long before it manifests itself on the outside. Your image is a direct correlation to how you think and what you believe about yourself.

As a speaker, I travel the country talking to audiences of women about branding, strategic marketing, vision planning, leadership and personal development. During one of my heavy travel periods I had literally traveled to the south, the mid-west, and the west, and at every stop women expressed the same resounding message, "I am not enough!" It broke my heart.

In small group discussions, times of sharing and one-on-one conversations, women were using different words but expressing the same sentiment. "I am not enough." They felt that because of things which had happened to them in their past, they had the belief that they weren't worthy and that they didn't have enough of what it takes to live their dreams and make an impact on the world with their gifts, talents and abilities.

My dear *DIVA-licious* woman entrepreneur, this is a way of thinking you must abandon and you must do it quickly. The thought of not being enough is the biggest lie you could ever believe about yourself. So many women have crafted an entire life around this one untruth, and it is costing millions of women the opportunity to live their best and most amazing life.

Set aside time to take an introspective look at yourself. Visit the wounded little girl on the inside who's controlling your life. That little wounded girl is running amuck and wrecking havoc over your future. It's time to have a heart to heart conversation with her and let her know that it's okay. You're okay. Let her know that you're a big girl now and you can handle what life throws your way. You don't need her to protect you anymore.

You have everything you need on the inside of you to live your dreams. You have the passion, the desire and the tenacity needed to start your business and turn it into a powerhouse brand. You are more than enough. There is no substitute for your gift in the world. You're not just enough, you are more than enough. Believe it. Say it. Act like it.

Fill in my G.A.P. (Goals Action Plan)

What changes do I need to implement?

What outcomes will I have in the next 30 days as a result?

YOU CAN'T
LOSE WITH THE
STUFF
"BOLD BUSINESS DIVAS" USE

THE RESOURCE LIST

Brand Strategy Consulting
www.IconicPersona.com
www.BrandWithCheryl.com

Social Media Sites
www.facebook.com
www.twitter.com
www.pinterest.com
www.linkedin.com

Domain registration
www.godaddy.com
www.cheapname.com

Trademark
www.uspto.gov

Recording software
www.audacity.com

Business Information Sources
www.sba.gov
www.score.org
www.entrepreneur.com
www.mashable.com
www.fastcompany.com
www.inc.com

Cloud Storage
www.dropbox.com
www.box.com
www.googledrive.com
www.mediafire.com
www.carbonite.com

Online image editor
www.picmonkey.com
www.lunapic.com

Screen capture
www.techsmith.com
www.screencastomatic.com

Graphic Design
www.canva.com
www.easil.com
www.fiverr.com

RECOMMENDED READING LIST FOR DIVAS DOING BUSINESS

1. The Holy Bible
2. Platform - Michael Hyatt
3. Be Your Own Boss - Melinda Emerson
4. Release Your Brilliance - Simon T. Bailey
5. S.K.I.R.T.S. in the Boardroom - Marshawn Evans
6. The Dream Giver - Bruce Wilkinson
7. 10 Spiritual Principles of Successful Women - Victoria Lowe
8. Healing the Wounds of the Past – T. D. Jakes
9. E-Myth Mastery – Michael E. Gerber
10. 100 Ways to Simplify Your Life – Joyce Meyer
11. May I Have Your Attention Please – Mish Slade
12. The Success Principles – Jack Canfield
13. Purple Cow – Seth Godin
14. Principles of the Ultimate Business Diva – Kimmoly LaBoo
15. And for course…What Every DIVA Must Know About Starting Her Own Business – Cheryl Pullins, The Icon of Branding

These books are recommended from my personal library, and have helped with both my personal development and business growth.

A Letter to you, Bold Business Diva

Dear Bold Business Diva,

Getting to the end of this book signifies the beginning of something amazing for you, your business and your life.

Your vision, your value and your voice are all so powerful, but you have muffled the impact of their brilliance by being a "me too" brand. You have followed, watched, copied, mimicked and studied others for far too long. It's time for you to emerge with your iconic flavor, in confidence and power.

Don't underestimate the power of what makes you distinct and unduplicatable. The world needs it. The world needs you.

I know you may be thinking there are so many people saying and doing the same thing I want to say and do, which could be true, but no one can say it like you! Do it like you or be you.

Yes, there is a ton of content available for you so that you don't have to reinvent the wheel, but the rest has to be all you DIVA...all you! That's what people want. They want your fabulousness, so give it to them!

The world is waiting.

Much love, Cheryl

www.ingramcontent.com/pod-product-compliance
Lightning Source LLC
Chambersburg PA
CBHW071159090426
42736CB00012B/2390